Spirit:

Cocktail Name:

Type:

Ingredients:

Garnish:

Mixing Method:

Glass:

Additional Notes:

Spirit: ....

Cocktail Name: ....

Type: ....

Ingredients:

....

....

....

....

....

....

....

Garnish: ....

Mixing Method:

....

....

....

....

....

Glass:

Additional Notes:

....

....

Spirit: ....

Cocktail Name: ....

Type: ....

Ingredients:

....
....
....
....
....
....
....

Garnish: ....

Mixing Method:

....
....
....
....
....
....
....

Glass:

Additional Notes:

....
....

Spirit: ....

Cocktail Name: ....

Type: ....

Ingredients:

....
....
....
....
....
....
....

Garnish: ....

Mixing Method:

....
....
....
....
....
....

Glass:

Additional Notes:

....
....

Spirit: ....

Cocktail Name: ....

Type: ....

Ingredients:

.... | ....

.... | ....

.... | ....

.... | ....

.... | ....

.... | ....

.... | ....

Garnish: ....

Mixing Method:

....

....

....

....

....

....

Glass:

Additional Notes:

....

....

Spirit: ....

Cocktail Name: ....

Type: ....

Ingredients:

....

....

....

....

....

....

Garnish: ....

Mixing Method:

....

....

....

....

....

....

Glass:

Additional Notes:

....

....

Spirit: ....

Cocktail Name: ....

Type: ....

Ingredients:

....
....
....
....
....
....
....

Garnish: ....

Mixing Method:

....
....
....
....
....
....

Glass:

Additional Notes:

....
....

Spirit: ....

Cocktail Name: ....

Type: ....

Ingredients:

....

....

....

....

....

....

....

Garnish: ....

Mixing Method:

....

....

....

....

....

....

Glass:

Additional Notes:

....

....

Spirit:

Cocktail Name:

Type:

Ingredients:

Garnish:

Mixing Method:

Glass:

Additional Notes:

Spirit: ....

Cocktail Name: ....

Type: ....

Ingredients:

....

....

....

....

....

....

....

Garnish: ....

Mixing Method:

....

....

....

....

....

....

Glass:

Additional Notes:

....

....

Spirit:

Cocktail Name:

Type:

Ingredients:

Garnish:

Mixing Method:

Glass:

Additional Notes:

Spirit: ....

Cocktail Name: ....

Type: ....

Ingredients:

....

....

....

....

....

....

....

....

Garnish: ....

Mixing Method:

....

....

....

....

....

....

Glass:

Additional Notes:

....

....

Spirit: ....

Cocktail Name: ....

Type: ....

Ingredients:

....

....

....

....

....

....

....

....

Garnish: ....

Mixing Method:

....

....

....

....

....

....

Glass:

Additional Notes:

....

....

Spirit: ....

Cocktail Name: ....

Type: ....

Ingredients:

....

....

....

....

....

....

....

Garnish: ....

Mixing Method:

....

....

....

....

....

....

Glass:

Additional Notes:

....

....

Spirit:

Cocktail Name:

Type:

Ingredients:

Garnish:

Mixing Method:

Glass:

Additional Notes:

Spirit: ....

Cocktail Name: ....

Type: ....

Ingredients:

....

....

....

....

....

....

....

Garnish: ....

Mixing Method:

....

....

....

....

....

....

Glass:

Additional Notes:

....

....

Spirit:

Cocktail Name:

Type:

Ingredients:

Garnish:

Mixing Method:

Glass:

Additional Notes:

Spirit: ....

Cocktail Name: ....

Type: ....

Ingredients:

....

....

....

....

....

....

....

Garnish: ....

Mixing Method:

....

....

....

....

....

....

Glass:

Additional Notes:

....

....

Spirit:

Cocktail Name:

Type:

Ingredients:

Garnish:

Mixing Method:

Glass:

Additional Notes:

Spirit: ....

Cocktail Name: ....

Type: ....

Ingredients:

....

....

....

....

....

....

....

Garnish: ....

Mixing Method:

....

....

....

....

....

....

Glass:

Additional Notes:

....

....

Spirit: ....

Cocktail Name: ....

Type: ....

Ingredients:

....
....
....
....
....
....
....

Garnish: ....

Mixing Method:

....
....
....
....
....
....

Glass:

Additional Notes:

....
....

Spirit: ....

Cocktail Name: ....

Type: ....

Ingredients:

....
....
....
....
....
....

Garnish: ....

Mixing Method:

....

....

....

....

....

....

Glass:

Additional Notes:

....

....

Spirit:

Cocktail Name:

Type:

Ingredients:

Garnish:

Mixing Method:

Glass:

Additional Notes:

Spirit: ....

Cocktail Name: ....

Type: ....

Ingredients:

....

....

....

....

....

....

....

Garnish: ....

Mixing Method:

....

....

....

....

....

....

Glass:

Additional Notes:

....

....

Spirit: ....

Cocktail Name: ....

Type: ....

Ingredients:

....

....

....

....

....

....

....

Garnish: ....

Mixing Method:

....

....

....

....

....

....

Glass:

Additional Notes:

....

....

Spirit: ....

Cocktail Name: ....

Type: ....

Ingredients:

....

....

....

....

....

....

....

Garnish: ....

Mixing Method:

....

....

....

....

....

....

Glass:

Additional Notes:

....

....

Spirit: ....

Cocktail Name: ....

Type: ....

Ingredients:

....
....
....
....
....
....
....

Garnish: ....

Mixing Method:

....
....
....
....
....
....

Glass:

Additional Notes:

....
....

Spirit:

Cocktail Name:

Type:

Ingredients:

Garnish:

Mixing Method:

Glass:

Additional Notes:

Spirit:

Cocktail Name:

Type:

Ingredients:

Garnish:

Mixing Method:

Glass:

Additional Notes:

Spirit: ....

Cocktail Name: ....

Type: ....

Ingredients:

....

....

....

....

....

....

....

Garnish: ....

Mixing Method:

....

....

....

....

....

....

Glass:

Additional Notes:

....

....

Spirit:

Cocktail Name:

Type:

Ingredients:

Garnish:

Mixing Method:

Glass:

Additional Notes:

Spirit: ....

Cocktail Name: ....

Type: ....

Ingredients:

....
....
....
....
....
....
....

Garnish: ....

Mixing Method:

....
....
....
....
....
....
....

Glass:

Additional Notes:

....
....

Spirit: ....

Cocktail Name: ....

Type: ....

Ingredients:

....

....

....

....

....

....

Garnish: ....

Mixing Method:

....

....

....

....

....

....

....

Glass:

Additional Notes:

....

....

Spirit:

Cocktail Name:

Type:

Ingredients:

Garnish:

Mixing Method:

Glass:

Additional Notes:

Spirit: ....

Cocktail Name: ....

Type: ....

Ingredients:

....

....

....

....

....

....

....

Garnish: ....

Mixing Method:

....

....

....

....

....

Glass:

Additional Notes:

....

....

Spirit:

Cocktail Name:

Type:

Ingredients:

Garnish:

Mixing Method:

Glass:

Additional Notes:

Spirit: ....

Cocktail Name: ....

Type: ....

Ingredients:

.... | ....

.... | ....

.... | ....

.... | ....

.... | ....

.... | ....

.... | ....

Garnish: ....

Mixing Method:

....

....

....

....

....

....

Glass:

Additional Notes:

....

....

Spirit: ....

Cocktail Name: ....

Type: ....

Ingredients:

....
....
....
....
....
....
....

Garnish: ....

Mixing Method:

....
....
....
....
....
....

Glass:

Additional Notes:

....
....

Spirit:

Cocktail Name:

Type:

Ingredients:

Garnish:

Mixing Method:

Glass:

Additional Notes:

Spirit: ....

Cocktail Name: ....

Type: ....

Ingredients:

....

....

....

....

....

....

Garnish: ....

Mixing Method:

....

....

....

....

....

Glass:

Additional Notes:

....

....

Spirit: ....

Cocktail Name: ....

Type: ....

Ingredients:

....
....
....
....
....
....
....

Garnish: ....

Mixing Method:

....
....
....
....
....
....

Glass:

Additional Notes:

....
....

Spirit: ....

Cocktail Name: ....

Type: ....

Ingredients:

....
....
....
....
....
....

Garnish: ....

Mixing Method:

....
....
....
....
....
....

Glass:

Additional Notes:

....
....

Spirit: ....

Cocktail Name: ....

Type: ....

Ingredients:

....

....

....

....

....

....

....

Garnish: ....

Mixing Method:

....

....

....

....

....

....

....

Glass:

Additional Notes:

....

....

Spirit: ....

Cocktail Name: ....

Type: ....

Ingredients:

....

....

....

....

....

....

....

Garnish: ....

Mixing Method:

....

....

....

....

....

....

....

Glass:

Additional Notes:

....

....

Spirit:

Cocktail Name:

Type:

Ingredients:

Garnish:

Mixing Method:

Glass:

Additional Notes:

Spirit: ....

Cocktail Name: ....

Type: ....

Ingredients:

....
....
....
....
....
....
....

Garnish: ....

Mixing Method:

....
....
....
....
....
....

Glass:

Additional Notes:

....
....

Spirit: ....

Cocktail Name: ....

Type: ....

Ingredients:

....

....

....

....

....

....

....

Garnish: ....

Mixing Method:

....

....

....

....

....

....

Glass:

Additional Notes:

....

....

Spirit: ....

Cocktail Name: ....

Type: ....

Ingredients:

.... | ....
.... | ....
.... | ....
.... | ....
.... | ....
.... | ....

Garnish: ....

Mixing Method:

....

....

....

....

....

....

Glass:

Additional Notes:

....

....

Spirit: ....

Cocktail Name: ....

Type: ....

Ingredients:

.... | ....
.... | ....
.... | ....
.... | ....
.... | ....
.... | ....

Garnish: ....

Mixing Method:

....
....
....
....
....
....

Glass:

Additional Notes:

....
....

Spirit: ....

Cocktail Name: ....

Type: ....

Ingredients:

....
....
....
....
....
....
....

Garnish: ....

Mixing Method:

....
....
....
....
....
....

Glass:

Additional Notes:

....
....

Spirit: ....

Cocktail Name: ....

Type: ....

Ingredients:

....
....
....
....
....
....
....

Garnish: ....

Mixing Method:

....
....
....
....
....
....

Glass:

Additional Notes:

....
....

Spirit:

Cocktail Name:

Type:

Ingredients:

Garnish:

Mixing Method:

Glass:

Additional Notes:

Spirit: ....

Cocktail Name: ....

Type: ....

Ingredients:

....

....

....

....

....

....

....

Garnish: ....

Mixing Method: ....

....

....

....

....

....

....

Glass:

Additional Notes:

....

....

Spirit:

Cocktail Name:

Type:

Ingredients:

Garnish:

Mixing Method:

Glass:

Additional Notes:

Spirit: ....

Cocktail Name: ....

Type: ....

Ingredients:

....
....
....
....
....
....
....

Garnish: ....

Mixing Method:

....
....
....
....
....
....
....

Glass:

Additional Notes:

....
....

Spirit:

Cocktail Name:

Type:

Ingredients:

Garnish:

Mixing Method:

Glass:

Additional Notes:

Spirit:

Cocktail Name:

Type:

Ingredients:

Garnish:

Mixing Method:

Glass:

Additional Notes:

Spirit: ....

Cocktail Name: ....

Type: ....

Ingredients:

....

....

....

....

....

....

Garnish: ....

Mixing Method:

....

....

....

....

....

....

Glass:

Additional Notes:

....

....

Spirit:

Cocktail Name:

Type:

Ingredients:

Garnish:

Mixing Method:

Glass:

Additional Notes:

Spirit: ....

Cocktail Name: ....

Type: ....

Ingredients:

....

....

....

....

....

....

....

Garnish: ....

Mixing Method:

....

....

....

....

....

....

Glass:

Additional Notes:

....

....

Spirit: ....

Cocktail Name: ....

Type: ....

Ingredients:

....
....
....
....
....
....
....

Garnish: ....

Mixing Method:

....
....
....
....
....
....

Glass:

Additional Notes:

....
....

Spirit: ....

Cocktail Name: ....

Type: ....

Ingredients:

....
....
....
....
....
....
....

Garnish: ....

Mixing Method:

....
....
....
....
....
....

Glass:

Additional Notes:

....
....

Spirit: ....

Cocktail Name: ....

Type: ....

Ingredients:

....

....

....

....

....

....

....

Garnish: ....

Mixing Method:

....

....

....

....

....

....

Glass:

Additional Notes:

....

....

Spirit: ....

Cocktail Name: ....

Type: ....

Ingredients:

....

....

....

....

....

....

....

Garnish: ....

Mixing Method:

....

....

....

....

....

....

....

Glass:

Additional Notes:

....

....

Spirit: ....

Cocktail Name: ....

Type: ....

Ingredients:

....
....
....
....
....
....
....

Garnish: ....

Mixing Method:

....
....
....
....
....
....

Glass:

Additional Notes:

....
....

Spirit:

Cocktail Name:

Type:

Ingredients:

Garnish:

Mixing Method:

Glass:

Additional Notes:

Spirit:

Cocktail Name:

Type:

Ingredients:

Garnish:

Mixing Method:

Glass:

Additional Notes:

Spirit: ....

Cocktail Name: ....

Type: ....

Ingredients:

....
....
....
....
....
....
....

Garnish: ....

Mixing Method:

....
....
....
....
....
....

Glass:

Additional Notes:

....
....

Spirit: ....

Cocktail Name: ....

Type: ....

Ingredients:

....

....

....

....

....

....

....

Garnish: ....

Mixing Method:

....

....

....

....

....

....

Glass:

Additional Notes:

....

....

Spirit: ....

Cocktail Name: ....

Type: ....

Ingredients:

....

....

....

....

....

....

....

Garnish: ....

Mixing Method:

....

....

....

....

....

....

Glass:

Additional Notes:

....

....

Spirit: ....

Cocktail Name: ....

Type: ....

Ingredients:

....

....

....

....

....

....

....

Garnish: ....

Mixing Method:

....

....

....

....

....

....

Glass:

Additional Notes:

....

....

Spirit: ....

Cocktail Name: ....

Type: ....

Ingredients:

....

....

....

....

....

....

....

Garnish: ....

Mixing Method:

....

....

....

....

....

....

Glass:

Additional Notes:

....

....

Spirit: ....

Cocktail Name: ....

Type: ....

Ingredients:

....
....
....
....
....
....
....

Garnish: ....

Mixing Method:

....
....
....
....
....
....

Glass:

Additional Notes:

....
....

Spirit: ....

Cocktail Name: ....

Type: ....

Ingredients:

....
....
....
....
....
....
....

Garnish: ....

Mixing Method:

....
....
....
....
....
....

Glass:

Additional Notes:

....
....

Spirit: ....

Cocktail Name: ....

Type: ....

Ingredients:

....

....

....

....

....

....

....

Garnish: ....

Mixing Method:

....

....

....

....

....

....

Glass:

Additional Notes:

....

....

Spirit: ....

Cocktail Name: ....

Type: ....

Ingredients:

....
....
....
....
....
....
....

Garnish: ....

Mixing Method:

....
....
....
....
....
....
....

Glass:

Additional Notes:

....
....

Spirit: ....

Cocktail Name: ....

Type: ....

Ingredients:

....

....

....

....

....

....

....

Garnish: ....

Mixing Method:

....

....

....

....

....

Glass:

Additional Notes:

....

....

Spirit: ....

Cocktail Name: ....

Type: ....

Ingredients:

....

....

....

....

....

....

....

Garnish: ....

Mixing Method:

....

....

....

....

....

....

Glass:

Additional Notes:

....

....

Spirit: ....

Cocktail Name: ....

Type: ....

Ingredients:

....

....

....

....

....

....

....

Garnish: ....

Mixing Method:

....

....

....

....

....

Glass:

Additional Notes:

....

....

Spirit: ....

Cocktail Name: ....

Type: ....

Ingredients:

....
....
....
....
....
....
....

Garnish: ....

Mixing Method:

....
....
....
....
....
....

Glass:

Additional Notes:

....
....

Spirit:

Cocktail Name:

Type:

Ingredients:

Garnish:

Mixing Method:

Glass:

Additional Notes:

Spirit: ....

Cocktail Name: ....

Type: ....

Ingredients:

....

....

....

....

....

....

....

Garnish: ....

Mixing Method:

....

....

....

....

....

....

....

Glass:

Additional Notes:

....

....

Spirit: ....

Cocktail Name: ....

Type: ....

Ingredients:

....

....

....

....

....

....

....

Garnish: ....

Mixing Method:

....

....

....

....

....

....

Glass:

Additional Notes:

....

....

Spirit: ....

Cocktail Name: ....

Type: ....

Ingredients:

....

....

....

....

....

....

....

Garnish: ....

Mixing Method:

....

....

....

....

....

....

Glass:

Additional Notes:

....

....

Spirit: ....

Cocktail Name: ....

Type: ....

Ingredients:

....
....
....
....
....
....
....

Garnish: ....

Mixing Method:

....
....
....
....
....
....

Glass:

Additional Notes:

....
....

Spirit: ....

Cocktail Name: ....

Type: ....

Ingredients:

....
....
....
....
....
....
....

Garnish: ....

Mixing Method:

....
....
....
....
....
....
....

Glass:

Additional Notes:

....
....

Spirit:

Cocktail Name:

Type:

Ingredients:

Garnish:

Mixing Method:

Glass:

Additional Notes:

Spirit: ....

Cocktail Name: ....

Type: ....

Ingredients:

....

....

....

....

....

....

....

Garnish: ....

Mixing Method:

....

....

....

....

....

....

....

Glass:

Additional Notes:

....

....

Spirit: ....

Cocktail Name: ....

Type: ....

Ingredients:

....

....

....

....

....

....

....

Garnish: ....

Mixing Method:

....

....

....

....

....

....

Glass:

Additional Notes:

....

....

Spirit:

Cocktail Name:

Type:

Ingredients:

Garnish:

Mixing Method:

Glass:

Additional Notes:

Spirit: ....

Cocktail Name: ....

Type: ....

Ingredients:

....

....

....

....

....

....

....

Garnish: ....

Mixing Method:

....

....

....

....

....

....

Glass:

Additional Notes:

....

....

Spirit:

Cocktail Name:

Type:

Ingredients:

Garnish:

Mixing Method:

Glass:

Additional Notes:

Spirit:

Cocktail Name:

Type:

Ingredients:

Garnish:

Mixing Method:

Glass:

Additional Notes:

Spirit: ....

Cocktail Name: ....

Type: ....

Ingredients:

....

....

....

....

....

....

....

Garnish: ....

Mixing Method:

....

....

....

....

....

....

Glass:

Additional Notes:

....

....

Spirit: ....

Cocktail Name: ....

Type: ....

Ingredients:

....
....
....
....
....
....
....

Garnish: ....

Mixing Method:

....
....
....
....
....
....

Glass:

Additional Notes:

....
....

Spirit: ....

Cocktail Name: ....

Type: ....

Ingredients:

....
....
....
....
....
....
....

Garnish: ....

Mixing Method:

....
....
....
....
....
....

Glass:

Additional Notes:

....
....

Spirit: ....

Cocktail Name: ....

Type: ....

Ingredients:

....

....

....

....

....

....

....

Garnish: ....

Mixing Method:

....

....

....

....

....

Glass:

Additional Notes:

....

....

Spirit: ....

Cocktail Name: ....

Type: ....

Ingredients:

....
....
....
....
....
....
....

Garnish: ....

Mixing Method:

....
....
....
....
....
....

Glass:

Additional Notes:

....
....

Spirit: ....

Cocktail Name: ....

Type: ....

Ingredients:

....

....

....

....

....

....

Garnish: ....

Mixing Method:

....

....

....

....

....

....

Glass:

Additional Notes:

....

....

Spirit: ....

Cocktail Name: ....

Type: ....

Ingredients:

....
....
....
....
....
....
....

Garnish: ....

Mixing Method:

....
....
....
....
....

Glass:

Additional Notes:

....
....

Spirit:

Cocktail Name:

Type:

Ingredients:

Garnish:

Mixing Method:

Glass:

Additional Notes:

Spirit: ....

Cocktail Name: ....

Type: ....

Ingredients:

....

....

....

....

....

....

....

Garnish: ....

Mixing Method:

....

....

....

....

....

Glass:

Additional Notes:

....

....

Spirit: ....

Cocktail Name: ....

Type: ....

Ingredients:

....

....

....

....

....

....

Garnish: ....

Mixing Method:

....

....

....

....

....

....

Glass:

Additional Notes:

....

....

Spirit: ....

Cocktail Name: ....

Type: ....

Ingredients:

....
....
....
....
....
....
....

Garnish: ....

Mixing Method:

....
....
....
....
....
....
....

Glass:

Additional Notes:

....
....

Spirit: ....

Cocktail Name: ....

Type: ....

Ingredients:

....

....

....

....

....

....

....

Garnish: ....

Mixing Method:

....

....

....

....

....

....

....

Glass:

Additional Notes:

....

....

Spirit: ....

Cocktail Name: ....

Type: ....

Ingredients:

....

....

....

....

....

....

....

Garnish: ....

Mixing Method:

....

....

....

....

....

....

Glass:

Additional Notes:

....

....

Spirit: ....

Cocktail Name: ....

Type: ....

Ingredients:

....

....

....

....

....

....

....

Garnish: ....

Mixing Method:

....

....

....

....

....

....

Glass:

Additional Notes:

....

....

Spirit:

Cocktail Name:

Type:

Ingredients:

Garnish:

Mixing Method:

Glass:

Additional Notes:

Spirit: ....

Cocktail Name: ....

Type: ....

Ingredients:

....

....

....

....

....

....

....

Garnish: ....

Mixing Method:

....

....

....

....

....

Glass:

Additional Notes:

....

....

Spirit: ....

Cocktail Name: ....

Type: ....

Ingredients:

....
....
....
....
....
....
....

Garnish: ....

Mixing Method:

....
....
....
....
....
....

Glass:

Additional Notes:

....
....

Spirit: ....

Cocktail Name: ....

Type: ....

Ingredients:

....
....
....
....
....
....
....

Garnish: ....

Mixing Method:

....
....
....
....
....
....

Glass:

Additional Notes:

....
....

Spirit: ....

Cocktail Name: ....

Type: ....

Ingredients:

....

....

....

....

....

....

Garnish: ....

Mixing Method:

....

....

....

....

....

....

Glass:

Additional Notes:

....

....

Spirit: ....

Cocktail Name: ....

Type: ....

Ingredients:

....

....

....

....

....

....

....

....

Garnish: ....

Mixing Method:

....

....

....

....

....

....

Glass:

Additional Notes:

....

....

Spirit: ....

Cocktail Name: ....

Type: ....

Ingredients:

....

....

....

....

....

....

Garnish: ....

Mixing Method:

....

....

....

....

....

....

....

Glass:

Additional Notes:

....

....

Spirit:

Cocktail Name:

Type:

Ingredients:

Garnish:

Mixing Method:

Glass:

Additional Notes:

Spirit: ....

Cocktail Name: ....

Type: ....

Ingredients:

....

....

....

....

....

....

....

Garnish: ....

Mixing Method:

....

....

....

....

....

....

Glass:

Additional Notes:

....

....

Spirit:

Cocktail Name:

Type:

Ingredients:

Garnish:

Mixing Method:

Glass:

Additional Notes:

Spirit: ....

Cocktail Name: ....

Type: ....

Ingredients:

....

....

....

....

....

....

....

Garnish: ....

Mixing Method:

....

....

....

....

....

....

Glass:

Additional Notes:

....

....

Spirit:

Cocktail Name:

Type:

Ingredients:

Garnish:

Mixing Method:

Glass:

Additional Notes:

Spirit:

Cocktail Name:

Type:

Ingredients:

Garnish:

Mixing Method:

Glass:

Additional Notes:

Made in United States
Troutdale, OR
12/22/2023

16347923R00070